W9-ATF-112

DATE DUE

Malaysia

For their help in the preparation of *Children of the World: Malaysia*, the editors gratefully thank Roslan Ariff, Milwaukee, Wis.; the Embassy of Malaysia (Canada), Ottawa, Ont.; the Embassy of Malaysia (U.S.), Washington, D.C.; the International Institute of Wisconsin, Milwaukee; and the United States Department of State, Bureau of Public Affairs, Office of Public Communication, Washington, D.C., for unencumbered use of material in the public domain. A special thanks to Roslan Ariff, Chee Wai Fung, Hasni Mukhtar, Khay Khong, Noorlelawati Hashim, Osman Nasir, Poh Choo Chuah, and Zainordin Basiron, all students at the University of Wisconsin-Milwaukee, for their time, humor, and good will.

Library of Congress Cataloging-in-Publication Data

Oshihara, Yuzuru.
   Malaysia.

   (Children of the world)
   Includes index.
   Summary: Introduces the country of Malaysia through a look at the life of eleven-year-old Widiyati who lives with her grandparents in a small village on the island of Penang.
   1. Malaysia—Juvenile literature. 2. Children—Malaysia—Juvenile literature. [1. Malaysia. 2. Family life—Malaysia] I. Knowlton, MaryLee, 1946- . II. Sachner, Mark, 1948- III. Series: Children of the world (Milwaukee, Wis.)
DS592.O73 1987   959.5   86-42802

ISBN 1-55532-185-2
ISBN 1-55532-160-7 (lib. bdg.)

North American edition first published in 1987 by

Gareth Stevens, Inc.
7221 West Green Tree Road   Milwaukee, Wisconsin 53223, USA

This work was originally published in shortened form consisting of section I only.
Photography on page 59 by Leanne Dillingham.
Photographs and original text copyright © 1986 by Yuzuru Oshihara.
First and originally published by Kaisei-sha Publishing Co., Ltd., Tokyo.
World English rights arranged with Kaisei-sha Publishing Co., Ltd. through Japan Foreign-Rights Centre.

Typeset by Ries Graphics ltd., Milwaukee.
Design: Leanne Dillingham & Laurie Shock.
Map design: Gary Moseley.

1 2 3 4 5 6 7 8 9 9 92 91 90 89 88 87

Children of the World

Malaysia

Photography
by Yuzuro Oshihara

Edited by
MaryLee Knowlton &
Mark J. Sachner

Gareth Stevens Publishing
Milwaukee

. . . a note about *Children of the World:*

The children of the world live in fishing towns and urban centers, on islands and in
mountain valleys, on sheep ranches and fruit farms. This series follows one child in
each country through the pattern of his or her life. Candid photographs show the children
with their families, at school, at play, and in their communities. The text describes the
dreams of the children and, often through their own words, tells how they see themselves
and their lives.

Each book also explores events that are unique to the country in which the child lives,
including festivals, religious ceremonies, and national holidays. The *Children of the World*
series does more than tell about foreign countries. It introduces the children of each country
and shows readers what it is like to be a child in that country.

. . . and about *Malayasia:*

Eleven-year-old Widiyati lives with her grandparents in the small village of Sungai Rusa on
the island of Penang. Her parents have been in the United States for four years while her
father studies there, and Yati is preparing for their return. With her grandfather, who is the
village headman, she shops, cooks, and watches him attend to village affairs.

To enhance this book's value in libraries and classrooms, comprehensive reference sections
include up-to-date data about Malaysia's geography, demographics, language, currency,
education, culture, industry, and natural resources. *Malaysia* also features a bibliography,
research topics, activity projects, and discussions of such subjects as Kuala Lumpur, the
country's history, political system, ethnic and religious composition, and language.

The living conditions and experiences of children in Malaysia vary tremendously according to
economic, environmental, and ethnic circumstances. The reference sections help bring to
life for young readers the diversity and richness of the culture and heritage of Malaysia. Of
particular interest are discussions of the relations between the Malays and other indigenous
minority cultures in Malaysia, principally Chinese and Indian, all of whom have made their
presence felt in the language and traditions of Malaysia.

CONTENTS

LIVING IN MALAYSIA:
Yati, a Girl and Her Grandparents

Yati's family: Yati, her mother, her younger sister Malini, Grandpa, Grandma, her older sister Nora, her younger brother Fatihi, and her father.

Yati is an eleven-year-old girl from the island of Penang in Malaysia. Her whole name is very long — Widiyati binti Shaik Ahmad Soekarno. It means Widiyati, the daughter of Shaik Ahmad Soekarno, her father. Her family is Malay, one of the peoples of Malaysia. They are Muslim.

Yati was born in Kuala Lumpur, the capital of Malaysia. Four years ago her parents and younger brother went to the United States. Her father has been studying at Columbia University in New York. Yati stayed in Malaysia. She lives with her grandparents in the village of Sungai Rusa.

The house where Yati lives. It is fancier than most of the others in the village.

The island of Penang attracts many tourists. But Sungai Rusa is on the other side of the island, away from the hotels. The village gets its name from the Sungai Rusa, or *Deer River*. This is a small river that runs through the village. It is a quiet village with few cars. Yati can go most anywhere by bicycle.

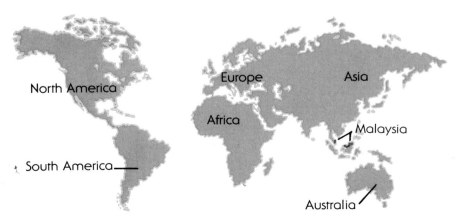

Shopping with Grandpa.

Yati's Grandma and Grandpa

Yati's Grandpa is 70 years old. He used to be principal of Yati's elementary school. Now he is the village *ketua,* or headman. He is active in village politics and goes to many meetings.

Yati's grandfather's name is Haji Ashari. *Haji* is the name for a Muslim man who has taken a trip to Mecca in Saudi Arabia. Mecca is a holy city for Muslims. The special trip is called a pilgrimage. A woman who has been on this pilgrimage is called *Hajah.*

Haji Ashari is a very busy man. But he takes Yati with him to many of his meetings and appointments. He drives her to school and takes her shopping. They're always together.

Grandpa at work. As village headman, he is very busy.

Grandpa drives Yati into nearby Balik Pulau.

Grandpa when he was a teacher at Yati's school.

Yati washes the dishes after meals.

Yati's Grandma has a lot of pain in her legs, so Yati helps her with many of her chores. She sets the table and clears it after meals. Then she washes the dishes. She tidies the yard around the house and feeds the chickens. In the evening, she chases them into the coop. They never want to go in, and Yati often has to chase them around the house a few times.

Her Grandma does the cooking. In the morning they have bread, tea, and salad. Yati brews the tea. For lunch and dinner they often eat curried chicken or beef. It is served with rice boiled in coconut milk.

Making a crushed-peanuts-and-cream cake with Grandpa.

The waters around the island of Penang have lots of fish. That is Yati's favorite food. Chinese and Indian Malaysians also eat pork, but Muslims do not. Muslims are unlike the other Malaysians in other ways, too. The Chinese, for example, eat with chopsticks. But Yati and other Muslims eat only with their right hand. According to custom, the left hand is used for going to the bathroom, and the right hand is used for eating.

Putting the finished cake into the refrigerator to cool.

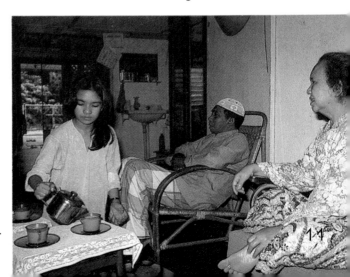
Serving Grandma and Uncle Ishak tea and cookies.

11

A meal with no eating utensils. Using only the right hand to tear off chicken meat, break up fish,

and carry rice to your mouth takes lots of practice. Yati has been at it a while, and she is quite good at it.

Hopscotch is a popular game among young Malaysian girls.

Yati and Her Friend Mazlinda

Most of Yati's friends live nearby. This is one of the things she loves about living in Sungai Rusa. Her best friend is Mazlinda. The two girls are in the same class at school. Today Mazlinda and Yati play a game called "chongkak." They play this game with stones and a board with rows of holes. Each player takes a turn and moves her stones one at a time. The winner is the one who gets all her stones into the hole on the right. Only the girls play this game. Yati and Mazlinda also play hopscotch. Yati is best at chongkak, but Mazlinda is better at hopscotch.

Playing chongkak with Mazlinda.

Because the weather is always warm in Malaysia, children play outside all year round. Yati, Mazlinda, and their friends dress in light clothes. They wear thongs, which they simply call slippers, on their feet. When they sit down to play or to rest, they take off their slippers and sit on them. This gives them a soft place to sit and helps keep their clothes clean!

After homework's done, Yati enjoys television. Like many Malaysians, she enjoys both Malaysian shows and American shows such as *Dallas, The A Team, Hawaii Five-O,* and *Magnum P.I.*

Yati's Home

More than anything, Yati treasures her diary. Of course, she records what happens to her every day. But she also writes many of her secret thoughts and dreams in it. She also is very proud of the notebooks and books which she has won as prizes for her work at school. Her third treasure is her cassette tape recorder. Her father sent her a Michael Jackson tape from the United States. He is one of her favorites. Her Malaysian favorite is Noreen Noor, who sings all her songs in the Malay language. Yati listens to her on the radio and on her cassette recorder.

Yati's desk. The telephone is a toy!

Yati also uses her tape recorder to send messages to her parents in New York. They send the tapes back with messages for her. Since they left, a baby sister has been born. Yati knows her only through pictures and the tapes her parents send. Yati feels as if she knows her already, and she can't wait to see her in person.

One of Yati's treasures: Her cassette recorder.

Coconut and papaya trees grow in Yati's backyard. After the coconuts turn brown, they begin to fall from the trees. Everybody walks around the trees when they are dropping their fruit, because the coconuts are hard and heavy.

Durians.

Coconuts.

Papayas.

Jack fruit.

Pineapple.

18

How to eat a durian: 1. Cut the top with a knife.

Everybody walks around the coconut trees when they are dropping their fruit, because the coconuts are hard and heavy. The "king of fruits" is the durian. It is rough and covered with prickles, and it smells like a rotting onion. It may not *sound* very good. But the fruit inside *tastes* delicious. It takes a lot of strength to cut the outer skin and pull out the fruit. Yati's grandmother has been teaching her to do it.

2. Pull the shell open.

3. Take out the segments.

4. Enjoy the rich taste of the segments inside.

Putting down a new carpet for Grandpa's guests.

All the houses in the village are built with raised floors. The lower part is open. Here people dry their clothes and store their bikes. The people live on the upper floor. Yati's grandfather designed and built his house 30 years ago. Because of his high position in the village, it is fancier than most houses. It has rooms both upstairs and downstairs.

The neighborhood women help prepare the food.

The upstairs is used only for company. Today the village religious committee is meeting here. The neighborhood women cook the food. Yati helps put down the carpet and carry the food upstairs. The guests are all men. The men and women never sit down to a meal together at a party. Today, the women talk in the kitchen as they prepare food for the guests.

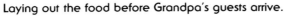

Laying out the food before Grandpa's guests arrive.

The meal has begun.

At Yati's house, there is no singing, dancing, or drinking of alcoholic beverages at social gatherings. Usually, the guests enjoy conversation over coffee, tea, and sweets. This is especially true at the meeting of the religious committee.

Washing the right hand with water before and after the meal.

The only food shop in Yati's village.

At Balik Pulau: hot bamboo cakes made with coconut flour.

At the Market

Yati and her Grandpa do the household shopping. It is a job they both love. The store in the village sells only canned food and spices. So once a week they drive to the nearby town of Balik Pulau. At the market there they buy fresh fish and vegetables.

Grandpa and Yati strike a deal in the marketplace.

23

Scenes from the market in Balik Pulau: Sugar cane juice.

Many Chinese live in Balik Pulau. They have stalls selling Chinese noodles, sugar cane juice, soy milk, and other Chinese products. Once a week the market sells clothes, groceries, tape cassettes, and Chinese medicine.

The fish market.

A fruit stall.

On that day the market is crowded. The market is an exciting place to be. Malaysians of many backgrounds and customs sell their wares. Yati loves seeing all the products and people.

The people in her village are all Malay Muslims. The Malays have lived on the Malay Peninsula since ancient times. They make up the largest race in Malaysia as a whole.

A general store with many canned goods.

Clothes stalls do a fast business.

In the market Yati sees members of the other cultures that make up the Malaysian population. They include Buddhist Chinese, Christian Chinese, and Hindu Indians.

Baking *roti canai* (Indian bread).

Yati and Her Friends at School

Yati is in the 6th grade at Sungai Rusa
Elementary School. The school is only a short
distance from her home, but her grandfather
drives her every day anyway. The road is
so busy in the morning that bicycles are
not allowed.

Yati is a class monitor. She is in charge of first
grade children at the morning flag assembly
and at lunch. She takes attendance and makes
sure everyone is standing neatly and quietly
in line.

Sungai Rusa Elementary School.

Mazlinda and Yati exchange their thoughts — and some food — before school.

School starts at 7:30. The day begins with a flag ceremony. The flag is raised, and the children sing a patriotic song. This morning they sing the national anthem. It is called "Negara-ku," or "My Homeland."

Yati's 6th grade class. The boys and girls sit on different sides of the room. Yati and Mazlinda sit at the front of the class.

The sixth grade is only one class, with 38 students. The boys sit on one side of the room, and the girls sit on the other side. The Muslim religion restricts the contact boys and girls can have with each other, especially as they get older.

Yati and Mazlinda like to sit next to each other. They also like to sit in the front of the class. This way they can pay close attention to the teacher and take part in class discussions.

Each day has eight or nine different lessons. Each lesson lasts 40 minutes. At mid day the children have a lunch break. The afternoon begins with another assembly. At this one, the principal talks to the students. Then the afternoon lessons begin.

The principal talks to the students at an assembly.

The first lesson today is physical education. The students don't change into special uniforms. Because the school has no gym, the class is held outside. The weather is so mild that the children can almost always play outside. The boys practice dribbling a soccer ball while the girls do free exercises and play catch.

Then it's back inside for arithmetic. The children are studying 5-figure multiplication and division. The rest of the plan for today will be history, art, English, handicrafts, and two lessons of language.

Physical education is always held outside.

The girls play catch in physical education.

Reading for school and fun in the library.

The village library.

Many varieties of fried foods.

Lots to choose from in the school courtyard.

Tempting baked goods.

The lunch break is at 11:00. Inside the school courtyard, village people sell food that they have prepared. Children and teachers can buy fried rice and fried noodles, each on a separate dish. Cakes and other baked foods are piled up for sale on large plates. There are also drinks and rice candy. Each food costs between 10 and 20 sen. This comes to about five cents.

Fried noodles are served on small dishes.

The girls usually bring juice or tea in a thermos from home, so they only buy food. Some children bring their lunch from home, too. Yati buys her lunch at school so she can have something different every day. Yati loves to sit with her friends and chat while they eat. This is her favorite time of the day at school.

The boys and girls enjoy their lunches together.

Yati listens carefully during English class.

Yati's favorite subjects are English, history, and science. She hopes to study at a British university. So she works hard to perfect her English. The British once ruled parts of the East Indies and Southeast Asia, including Malaysia. Therefore, English has become a universal language among the many races who live in Malaysia. Because only Malays go to Yati's school, the only foreign language is English. Schools with Chinese pupils teach Chinese, and schools with Indian pupils teach Tamil. In all the schools, however, teaching is conducted in the Malay language.

Yati's Malay language class.

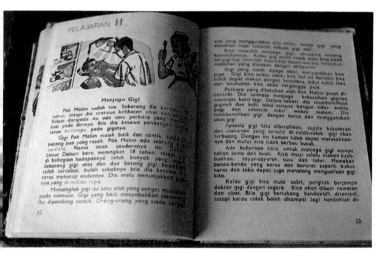

A Malay language textbook.

Yati became interested in history after she read "The Tale of Princess Mahsuri." It is a sad tale about a Malay princess who lived long ago on the island of Langkawi to the north of Penang. She was killed after being accused of adultery — a crime she hadn't committed. Legend has it that when she died, white blood flowed from her body. This was proof of her innocence. Her tomb is near the island town of Kuah.

Yati became interested in science after a teacher told her, "Everything in the world exists for a reason." Yati wants to know all the reasons.

Boys wear one style of uniform.

At the Sungai Rusa Elementary School, the children wear uniforms. For girls there are several styles. Islam teaches that girls should cover as much of their skin as possible. But families differ in thinking how much this should be. In strict Muslim families, girls must wear long skirts and scarves. Some families omit the scarf. Usually, young girls wear a blouse and jumper. Older girls wear a long skirt and scarf.

Girls from strict families wear long skirts and scarves.

Each lesson in a Malaysian school begins with the students saying "Assalam alaikum." This means "Peace and goodness be upon you" in Arabic. Everyone in Yati's class is Muslim and is learning Arabic words. At the end of the lesson they all say in Malay, "Terima kasih cikgu." This means "Thank you, teacher." Yati is a very serious student. She is at the top of her class. Her friend, Mazlinda, is second. Sometimes it's the other way around.

A uniform for a girl
from a fairly strict family.

A regular uniform for girls.

37

Going to Koran school in formal dress — a cap and long skirt.

Studying the Koran

After school, many of the children go to the mosque. Here an important man from the mosque speaks to the children. He tells them about praying, relations with friends, and what they should or should not do in their daily lives.

The Koran is read by following each word with a pointer.

Neighborhood children with their thick copies of the Koran. Day by day, Yati understands the holy text a little more.

Every night after dinner the neighborhood children gather at a nearby house. For an hour and a half they learn how to read the Koran, or *Quran*. The teachers are men of the village who can read the Koran well. The Koran is the most important holy text of Islam. It is written in Arabic, not Malay. At the age of six or seven, children learn how to read Arabic words. When they can read well enough, they begin reading the Koran. To read it all usually takes about five years. Yati will be through in about six more months.

Visiting Nora in Georgetown

When Yati and her grandfather say they are going to town, they mean Georgetown. Georgetown is on the other side of the island. Malaysia had once been a British colony. That is why Georgetown has an English name. Today more than half the residents are Chinese. Throughout Malaysia most Chinese live in the cities, and most Malays live in the countryside.

Yati's sister, Nora, lives in Georgetown with their other grandmother. Nora goes to secondary school there. Going to Georgetown is very special for Yati because it means she can see her sister.

Waiting for the bus.

Yati's Grandma's house in Georgetown. This is where her father grew up.

Nora and Grandma from Georgetown, and Yati and Grandpa from Sungai Rusa.

Family pictures hang on the walls.

42 The Georgetown bus. Malaysians are of many racial and ethnic backgrounds, including Malay, Chinese, and Indian.

Georgetown, Malaysia's second-largest city, after Kuala Lumpur. Many of its residents are Chinese, so a lot of the signs use Chinese characters.

Today their grandfather takes Yati and Nora shopping for shoes to go with their *baju kurong*. This is the traditional long dress worn by women. Yati and Nora's parents are coming back soon. When they last saw them, their daughters were just little girls. Now, wearing their long dresses, they will seem quite grown-up!

The baju kurong, a traditional Malaysian dress.

Yati finds a pair of shoes to go with her dress.

Together Again:
Good-bye Penang. Hello Kuala Lumpur!

The arrival at Penang Airport.

Today Yati's mother and father are coming home from the United States. She and her grandparents go to Penang airport to meet them. It has been four long years. She is very excited to see her little brother, Fatihi, again. And what a thrill it is to meet her new sister, Malini, who was born in the United States!

Presents from the U.S.: a stethoscope and a tonometer. Yati dreams of becoming a doctor some day.

Family pictures taken
before Yati's parents left for the U.S.

That evening: A long-awaited family reunion.

Now that the family is together again, Yati knows they will be going back to Kuala Lumpur. That means saying good-bye to her friends and school in Sungai Rusa. More than that, it means saying good-bye to her grandparents and the life they have shared for four years. Yati promises to come back as often as she can. This has been a special four years. She feels sad and, at the same time, very lucky.

FOR YOUR INFORMATION: Malaysia

Official name: Federation of Malaysia
Capital: Kuala Lumpur

History

Malaysia: A Varied Land, A Varied People

Malaysia is one country on two main bodies of land: the southern tip of the Malay Peninsula and the northern quarter of the island of Borneo. They are 400 miles (644 km) apart! The part on the Malay Peninsula is called West Malaysia, Malaya, and Peninsular Malaysia. The part on Borneo is called East Malaysia. Many countries and groups of people were on this land before it became known as Malaysia. Even today, Malaysia is made up of many different races and religions. All of them show something about the history of this country.

The Early Malay Kingdoms

The people of what is today Malaysia have lived — and often suffered — under colonial rule for centuries. Europeans first visited the Malay Peninsula in the 16th century. But hundreds of years before this, Malay people were already on the peninsula. It is thought that they may have come from the mainland of Asia. From the 9th to the 13th centuries, much of the Malay Peninsula was part of a Buddhist kingdom. In the 14th century, the Malay Peninsula became part of a Hindu kingdom. At first, the Malay kingdoms showed strong signs of East Indian culture. In the 13th and 14th centuries, however, merchants from Arabia and India came to Malaya. They brought Islam and Arabic to the peninsula. This migration began the conversion of Malays to Islam.

In the 15th century, the Kingdom of Malacca was formed on the Malay Peninsula. Malacca was ruled by a Muslim prince. It became the first unified society of Malays. Even today, Malay Muslims dominate Malaysian government and culture.

The Coming of the Europeans

In the 15th century, goods were shipped between India and China by water. Because of its place on this route, what is today Malaysia would be occupied by colonial powers and trading companies for centuries.

First Portugal (1511), then Holland (1641), and then Britain (1795) ruled Malacca. In fact, Britain would dominate the Malay Peninsula till 1941. In the late 18th century into the 19th and 20th centuries, Britain colonized Penang island, Singapore, the rest of Peninsular Malaysia (then known as Malaya), and northern Borneo.

A panoramic view of Georgetown on Penang island. Across the water is the mainland of Malaya (Peninsular Malaysia). In 1985, a bridge was built connecting Georgetown with the mainland.

Malaysia Today

The Japanese controlled the Malay Peninsula from 1941 till 1945. At that time the British once again took over. After World War II, Malays became fearful of growing Chinese and Indian influence on the peninsula. In 1948 Britain united its territories on the peninsula. They became the Federation, or Union, of Malaya. In 1957, Malaya became independent from Britain. In 1963, the present-day Federation of *Malaysia* was born with the addition of Singapore and of Sabah and Sarawak on Borneo. One other British colony in northern Borneo, Brunei, was also invited to join the Federation of Malaysia in 1963. It decided to stay under British rule.

Following the creation of Malaysia in 1963, war broke out between Malaysia and neighboring Indonesia. The government of Indonesian President Sukarno did not like the idea of a unified Malaysia. It was only the fall of his government in 1966 that brought friendly relations to these two countries.

With the addition of Singapore, Malaysia now had a city made up mostly of ethnic Chinese. In 1965 Singapore left the federation and became an independent nation. Singapore's withdrawal showed that the tensions between Malaysia's two main ethnic groups, the Malays and the Chinese, were as deep as ever.

The Boat People

At the end of the Vietnam War in 1975, North and South Vietnam became one country. In the South, many ethnic Chinese did not want to live under the new government. Some were property owners who did not want to give up their possessions to the communist government. Others feared persecution. Some of these people had to pay their way out. In North America, some churches and Vietnamese relatives sponsored new Vietnamese-Americans. But thousands of ethnic Chinese had to take refuge wherever they could.

49

Ethnic Chinese refugees from Vietnam, Cambodia, and Laos were scattered throughout Southeast Asia. Most fled to Thailand and Malaysia. Escape by water was very dangerous. Many boats were attacked by pirates in the Gulf of Siam, and thousands of refugees died. Hospital boats were set up off the island of Bidong, Malaysia, in the South China Sea. They were there to help refugees in need of medical attention. Also Malaysia set up a camp on Bidong. Malaysia would take care of the refugees until other countries gave them permanent asylum. The government also set up a school on Bidong. At this school, the refugees were taught English. The government felt that knowing English would help them get asylum in Western countries. But by the end of June, 1979, Malaysia had 76,000 refugees in the 30-acre (12-hectare) camp on Bidong. Malaysia felt it had to do something to make other countries help with the problem. Finally, the government announced that it would turn away ethnic Chinese from other countries.

This announcement made other countries take notice of what was going on. Within days, a special United Nations meeting took place in Geneva, Switzerland. It brought together 50 nations. They agreed to share responsibility for the fate of what had come to be known as the boat people. Some countries, including the U.S. and Canada, agreed to take in more refugees. Many countries promised financial help.

Despite these efforts, thousands of people are still in the camp on Bidong. The refugee problem has continued to result in agony and death for hundreds of thousands of people in Southeast Asia.

Population and Ethnic Groups

Malaysia has a population of about 15 million people. It is a country with many ethnic, racial, and religious groups. In fact, the official census lists over 50 ethnic groups! About 47% of the population is Malay, 35% Chinese, and 10% Indian. The remainder is made up of native minorities other than Malay. These minorities are mainly tribespeople in rural areas. They are a small minority in the country as a whole. But on the island of Borneo, they make up 50% of Sarawak's and 66% of Sabah's population. Together, the Malays and the non-Malay minorities other than Indian or Chinese are called *bumiputra*. This means "children of the soil." They make up about half the population of the country.

The Malays live throughout the country. They live mainly in the rural areas, although more and more have moved to the cities. They work as rice farmers, fishermen, or civil servants, and they are the main power in the government. The ethnic Chinese are mainly descendants of 19th century Chinese. The British brought them in as forced labor in the tin mines. When the British finally left Malaysia, the Chinese took over many of the businesses. Today, most live in the cities of the tin and rubber belt of West Malaysia, and they hold quite a bit of economic power. The Indians came, around the same time as the Chinese, from India, Pakistan, and Ceylon (now Sri Lanka). Like the Chinese, most Indians, too, were forced to work on the rubber plantations of Malaya (now Peninsular Malaysia). Most of Malaysia's ethnic Indians settled in Malaya. In addition to laboring on the rubber plantations, some have now gone into such professions as law.

Relations between ethnic Chinese and Malays have been strained since the 19th century. Today, the Malays hold nearly all of Malaysia's political power. And yet they are among the poorest of Malaysia's population. The Chinese, on the other hand, have greater economic power than any other group. And yet they have far less political power than the Malays. In 1969, race riots broke out in Malaysia. They were mainly between Malays and Chinese, and they did much to harm feelings between these two groups.

The government has tried to promote Malay language and culture. Many in the minority populations have responded favorably to this effort. But many have turned away from Malaysian concerns, back to the culture of their ancestors. Many ethnic Indians have rediscovered their traditional dances and music. Ethnic Chinese have begun to celebrate the festivals of their immigrant ancestors. The Chinese, Malays, and Indians all consider themselves Malaysians. Today they have ties through educational, sports, and cultural groups. Yet they tend to keep their own identities, and tensions between ethnic Chinese and Malays have been high.

Malaysia is still a new country that was ruled by others for centuries. Under Britain, the Malays, Chinese, and Indians were forced to compete for a better way of life. After being divided for so many years, Malaysians may need lots of time to feel united as one people.

A Chinese lion dance.

A Hindu temple in Georgetown. The style is East Indian.

Religion

Islam is the official national religion. But Malaysians may join any faith they choose. Most Malays are Muslims. The Chinese are mainly Buddhist. But many Chinese are Confucianist, Taoist, or Christian. Indians are mainly Hindu, with some Buddhists, Muslims, Sikhs, and Christians. Many non-Malay native minorities have adopted Islam, and some have become Christians. Many still follow their own ancient religious customs.

Government

Malaysia is a constitutional monarchy. It is made up of 13 states and the federal district of Kuala Lumpur. The states are governed by sultans who inherit their title. The monarch is elected to serve for five years. He is chosen from among the nine sultans of Peninsular Malaysia. Once elected, he is the leader of Islam in Malaysia, just as each of the sultans is the leader in his own state.

Actual executive power comes from a cabinet headed by the Prime Minister. The Prime Minister is the leader of the political party that wins the most seats in a parliamentary election. All adults in Malaysia may vote.

A major concern of Malaysia today is racial harmony. The government is trying to close the gap between the Chinese and Indians and the majority Malays. The Chinese hold great economic power, and the Malays, though poor, hold most of the power in government. With this in mind, the government gives priority in most fields to the Malays and to the other minorities whose origins are in Malaysia. This policy has excluded Chinese and others from many jobs and government programs.

Malaysia has been eager to make a good impression on foreign tourists and business people. To do this, the government has discouraged criticism of its policies. In recent years it has expelled foreign journalists who were critical of the government. The press is controlled by the government. Still, journalists feel it is much less oppressive than many other governments.

In the past, drug dealing has corrupted some parts of Malaysian society, economy, and government. The current government's drug policies are very severe. The penalty for illegal drug dealing is death. Malaysia received international attention in 1986 when it executed two young Australians for trying to export cocaine. Prime ministers from Australia and Britain appealed for the lives of the two men without success. Most Malaysians supported the executions. And they accused the Western governments of being concerned only because the two men were Westerners. They wondered why no one had protested the policy when Malaysia had executed Asians for the same crimes. Despite Western protest, Malaysia is committed to its drug program. Even the government's pamphlets promoting Malaysia as a place for tourists contain a prominent warning: "Trafficking of illegal drugs carries a death penalty."

Language

The official national language is Bahasa Malaysia. This is the language of the government and the schools. Its roots are Malay. But it is also a modern language, with many newly invented words. Everyone must learn Bahasa Malaysia, including Indians and Chinese. Also, the governments of Malaysia and Indonesia have decided to bring both countries' languages together in Bahasa. English is also widely used, especially in business and government. It is also taught in the schools. The Chinese also speak Chinese, in nine dialects. One commonly used dialect is Cantonese. Indians may speak one of seven Indian languages. The dialect depends on where their ancestors came from in India. Most Indians speak Tamil.

Arts and Crafts

The arts and crafts of Malaysia are rich and varied because of the many ethnic groups. Along the east coast of Malaya, puppeteers called To'Dalang act out classic Indian tales. The puppets are made from buffalo hide. In Kelantan, a theater troupe called Ma'Yong also presents dramas of old. These combine ballet, opera, drama, and comedy. They are accompanied by gongs, drums and other traditional instruments. Other theater productions include the Menora. All the performers are men, even in the women's roles. They wear grotesque masks and act out in dance ancient folktales. The dance consists of slow arm, leg, and finger movements. The music is supplied by an orchestra that plays drums, gongs, scrape instruments, and a woodwind called the Malay oboe.

Batik: One of Malaysia's traditional arts.

The newly dyed cloths are dried in the sun.

The arts and crafts of Malaysia also include beautiful textile products. Women make the *kain songket*. This is a lovely cloth handwoven with gold and silver threads. The cloth is used for formal ceremonies. *Batik* is a way of printing fabric. It uses wax to keep the dye from areas of the cloth. It is also a traditional Malaysian handicraft. The artist makes a design on cloth and covers with wax any area that should not be dyed. Then the cloth is dyed. After it is dyed, it is boiled to remove the wax. The artist repeats the process with the next layer of design, and the next. The more layers of dye, the more valuable the cloth. Malaysians make the cloth into dresses, tablecloths, napkins, bedsheets, and caftans. Women also weave leaves and bamboo strips into mats, hats, handbags, wallhangings, and baskets. First the leaves are split, cut, soaked, bleached, and dyed. They are then woven or braided into products.

In the past, silver was a luxury. It was found only in the royal courts. Rulers hired silversmiths to make items for their households and jewelry for the princes and princesses. Today skilled artists make pins, pendants, belts, rings, chains, jewelry boxes, and bowls for visitors and Malaysians with money. Woodcarving, leathercraft, and brasswork are also crafts that show the skills of the artists and craftspeople of Malaysia.

Land and Climate

Malaysia occupies two land regions in Southeast Asia. Part of it is on the southern half of the Malay Peninsula. The other part is in the northern quarter of the island of Borneo. The two parts are separated by about 400 miles (644 km) of the South China Sea.

Peninsular Malaysia is also known as West Malaysia or Malaya. Its area is about 51,000 sq. miles (132,000 sq. km). It is bordered by Thailand to the north, the South China Sea to the east, Singapore to the south, and the Strait of Malacca to the west. Across the narrow Strait of Malacca is the Indonesian island of Sumatra, or Sumatera.

The part of Malaysia in northern Borneo is known as East Malaysia. Its area is about 48,000 sq. miles (124,310 sq. km). The two states that make up this region are called Sarawak and Sabah. Under the British, Sabah was known as North Borneo. East Malaysia is bordered by the South China and Sulu Seas to the north, Brunei to the northeast, the Celebes Sea to the east, and the Kalimantan region of Indonesia to the south and west.

Malaysia's total area is about 127,000 sq. miles (330,000 sq. km). This makes Malaysia slightly larger than the state of New Mexico. About 90% of the total land is covered with dense forests. Most of these forests are on the jungle-covered mountains of the interior. Along the edges of the interior mountains are coastal plains.

A cut in a rubber tree oozes the white sap used in making rubber.

Malaysia is a tropical land of high temperatures and humidity and heavy rainfall. The average temperature is 80.6°F (27°C). Rainfall averages between 100 and 200 inches (2500 mm to 5000 mm) annually. The mountainous interior gets the heavier rains. Malaysia has two rainy seasons. Each is followed by a dry season. The Northeast monsoon season mainly affects East Malaysia and the east coast of West, or Peninsular, Malaysia. It runs from October through January. Some areas get 20 inches (500 mm) during January alone. The second rainy

Moving natural rubber through rollers to make it into sheets.

season is from May through September. This season is called the Southwest monsoon season. It affects mainly the west coast of Peninsular Malaysia.

A rice field near Sungai Rusa on Penang island.

Industry, Agriculture, and Natural Resources

By Southeast Asian standards, Malaysia has a very strong economy. It also has a high standard of living. Farming has always been the main strength of the economy, and about 40% of the people work in agriculture. Malaysia is the world's leading exporter of natural rubber (40% of the world's supply), palm oil (60%), tropical hardwood (37%), and peppers (42%). Even with these supplies of products, Malaysia still imports much of its food from other countries.

Throughout most of its history, Malaysia has also imported most of its manufactured goods. Malaysian industry has grown, however, and 30-35% of the people now work in industrial jobs. Leading industries include cars, metal products, electronics, rubber products, and textiles.

Malaysia's leading natural resources include oil, tin, timber, and copper. Malaysia is the world's largest exporter of tin. It provides 30% of the world's supply. In international trade, the U.S. is one of Malaysia's major markets. Malaysia sends 11% of all its exports to the U.S. — second to Japan (22%). And the U.S. also ranks second as Malaysia's supplier of imported goods — 15% to Japan's 25%. Canada ranks below 5% in its trade with Malaysia.

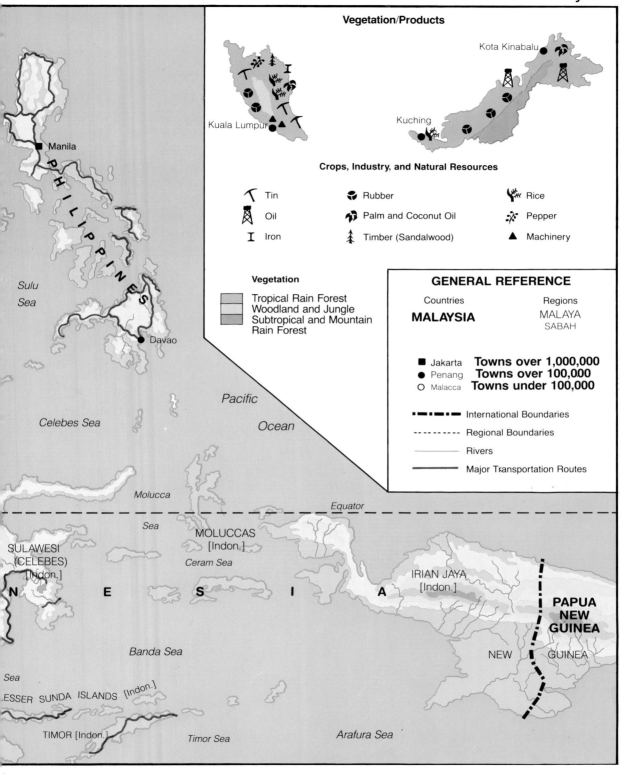

MALAYSIA — Political and Physical

Vegetation/Products

Kota Kinabalu

Kuala Lumpur

Kuching

Crops, Industry, and Natural Resources

Tin

Oil

Iron

Rubber

Palm and Coconut Oil

Timber (Sandalwood)

Rice

Pepper

Machinery

Vegetation

Tropical Rain Forest
Woodland and Jungle
Subtropical and Mountain
Rain Forest

GENERAL REFERENCE

Countries
MALAYSIA

Regions
MALAYA
SABAH

■ Jakarta **Towns over 1,000,000**
● Penang   **Towns over 100,000**
○ Malacca **Towns under 100,000**

International Boundaries

Regional Boundaries

Rivers

Major Transportation Routes

Manila

PHILIPPINES

Sulu
Sea

Davao

Celebes Sea

Pacific

Ocean

Molucca

Equator

Sea

MOLUCCAS
[Indon.]

Ceram Sea

IRIAN JAYA
[Indon.]

SULAWESI
(CELEBES)
[Indon.]

**PAPUA
NEW
GUINEA**

N   E   S   I   A

NEW   GUINEA

Banda Sea

Sea

LESSER SUNDA ISLANDS [Indon.]

TIMOR [Indon.]

Timor Sea

Arafura Sea

Education

Malaysians see education as a key to success, especially in improving one's social standing. The literacy rate in Malaysia is about 50%. But school is now compulsory for all primary grades (1-6) and three more secondary grades. This policy will improve the literacy rate greatly. After these nine years, all students take a public exam. This exam shows whether they may continue school for two more years, in either a secondary or a trade school.

There are seven universities in Malaysia. All of them are in West Malaysia. There are, however, some colleges in East Malaysia. Many of them are teacher-training colleges. Many Malaysians also go on to school in Australia, Britain, the United States, and other countries.

Some of these people remain in the countries in which they study. But the vast majority return to their own country and use their education there.

Sports and Recreation

Malaysians enjoy sports as both spectators and participants. These sports include soccer, badminton, ping-pong, basketball, field hockey, and *bersilat*, which is the Malay art of self-defense. The Chinese brought bersilat to Malaya in the 15th century. Some activities are linked both to Malaysia's colonial past and to its present as a tourist center. These include horseracing, bowling, golf, polo, tennis, and even gambling. Malaysians and tourists alike can share many other activities. These include hiking, bird-watching, jungle photography, surfing, fishing, scuba-diving, sailing, canoeing, and other outdoor activities. Malaysian theaters show mostly Malay, Chinese, and Indian movies.

In West Malaysia, local Malay customs include top spinning, bird singing contests, and kite flying. Top spinning is not just a game for children. Often the tops are as wide as dinner plates and can weigh as much as 15½ lbs (7 kg). Neighboring villages often hold contests, and some tops have been known to spin for as long as an hour and forty-five minutes! Bird singing contests are held in Kota Bharu. Each June, between 50 and 120 jungle birds perch on poles more than 29 ft (9 m) above the ground. They are specially trained for this competition. Kite flying had its beginnings in 16th century Malacca. Today, regular kite flying competitions are held after the harvest season. A kite, or *wau*, may be as long as 6 ft (1.8 m). It may have a wingspan as long as 8 ft (2.5 m). Each kite is judged by its altitude and design.

Currency

The main units of Malaysian currency are the *ringgit* and the *sen*. One ringgit = 100 sen. Two ringgit and fifty sen, or 2.5 ringgit, equal about one of our dollars.

Kuala Lumpur

Kuala Lumpur was once the capital of Selangor, a state on the west coast of Peninsular Malaysia (West Malaysia). In 1957, Kuala Lumpur became the federal capital of what is now Malaysia. Like the federal districts of Washington, D.C., and Mexico City, Kuala Lumpur is a federal territory. This means that it does not belong to any state. With a population of around one million, Kuala Lumpur is Malaysia's largest city. It is in an area that is rich in tin and rubber, and it was at first a tin mining center itself. Today it is a center for business, industry, transportation, higher education, and tourism. Kuala Lumpur is the home of several universities, and here, visitors can see both the new and the old of Malaysian culture and architecture. The capital's many sights include the National Mosque, Parliament, and the National Museum.

Kuala Lumpur also has signs of Malaysia's ethnic contrasts. In the center of town is a railway station with Arabian-style minarets, and on the riverfront is the old Chinese quarter with its street stalls. Just outside of town are sights that offer a contrast to Kuala Lumpur's busy city life: rubber plantations, tin mines, forests with monkeys and other animals, and the Batu Caves with their limestone stalagmites and stalactites.

Malaysians in North America

Most Malaysians who come to North America are here for a short time, usually as students. Very few become citizens of the United States or Canada. For example, in Canada, fewer than a thousand became citizens in 1983 and 1984 combined. Those who do become Canadians are mostly in technical jobs, such as computer science. In the United States, there are about 24,000 Malaysian students. But the

A group of Malaysian students at the University of Wisconsin-Milwaukee.

number of Malaysians who become U.S. citizens is very small — even smaller than in Canada. Most Malaysians who stay in the U.S. are professionals, such as engineers and architects. Most of these have gone to school in the U.S.

In both Canada and the U.S., there are more Malaysian immigrants in the West and Pacific Northwest — California in the U.S. and Vancouver, British Columbia, in Canada. Most Malaysians who immigrate to North America are ethnic Chinese. In Canada, for example, about 86% are Chinese. About 13% are Malaysian Indians, and fewer than one percent are Malays.

More Books About Malaysia

Here are more books about Malaysia. If you are interested in them, check your library. Some may be helpful in doing research for the ''Things to Do'' projects that follow.

Getting to Know Malaysia. King (Coward-McCann)
The Land and the People of Malaysia. Clifford (Lippincott)
Let's Visit Malaysia. Caldwell (John Day)
Take a Trip to Malaysia. Elder (Franklin Watts)

Glossary of Useful Malaysian Terms

Assalam alaikum
   (ah-sah-LAHM a-lay-KOOM) . . . . ''Peace and blessings be upon you'';
                                             Arabic greeting among Muslims
Bahasa (bah-HAH-sah) . . . . the ''artificial'' official language of
                                             Malaysia
baju (BAH-joo) . . . . a shirt or blouse
baju kurong (BAH-joo koo-RONG) . . . . . . a long traditional dress worn by women
batik (bah-TEEK) . . . . a kind of printing using cloth, dyes, and wax
bumiputra (boo-mee-POOH-trah) . . . . ''children of the soil''; Malays and non-
                                             Malay minorities other than Indians and
                                             Chinese
chongkak (CHONG-kok) . . . . a game played with stones, seeds, or
                                             beads on a board with holes in it
cik (cheek) . . . . Miss
cikgu (CHEEK-goo) . . . . teacher
dia (DEE-ah) . . . . she; he
encik (EN-cheek) . . . . Sir
halo, apa khabar?
   (hello, AH-pah kah-BAR) . . . . hello, how are you?
guru (GOO-roo) . . . . teacher
kain songket (cane song-KET) . . . . beautiful Malaysian cloth with gold and
                                             silver threads woven into it
ketua (KEH-too-ah) . . . . headman
negara (neh-GAH-rah) . . . . country; nation
orangutan (oh-RANG-hu-TAN) . . . . an ape with a reddish-brown coat, very
                                             long arms, and no tail; very common in
                                             Sabah and Sarawak, on Borneo (*orang
                                             hutan:* ''man of the forest'')
Quran (KUH-ran) . . . . Koran; holy text of Islam
roti canai (roh-TEE chah-NI) . . . . Indian bread
selamat pagi (seh-lah-MAHT PAH-gee) . . . good morning
selamat tinggal
   (sih-lah-MAHT ting-GAHL) . . . . good-bye
sila (SEE-lah) . . . . please
terima kasih (TREE-mah KAH-say) . . . . thank you
wau (WAH-ooh) . . . . kite

60

Things to Do — Research Projects

A country's laws can affect its relations with other countries. In 1986, for example, two Australians were executed in Malaysia for drug dealing. Their executions raised a cry of protest from Australia and Britain. Many Malaysians have wondered why Westerners do not protest this policy when it is carried out against Asians. They say that the governments of Britain and Australia acted only out of self-interest and showed more concern over the lives of Westerners than of Asians.

As you read about Malaysia, or any country, keep in mind the importance of having current information. Some of the research projects that follow need accurate, up-to-date information. That is why current newspapers and magazines are useful sources of information. Two publications your library may have will tell you about recent magazine and newspaper articles on many topics:

The Reader's Guide to Periodical Literature
Children's Magazine Guide

For accurate answers to questions about such topics of current interest as Malaysia's laws, ethnic and racial policies, and relations with other nations, look up *Malaysia* in these two publications. They will lead you to the most up-to-date information you can find.

1. How far is Penang, Malaysia, from where you live? Using maps, travel guides, travel agents, or any other resources you know of, find out how you could get there and how long it would take.

2. Besides Malays, Chinese, and Indians, Malaysia is home to many other ethnic groups. Here are some of them: Jakun, Kadazan, Bajau, Brunei, Murut, Suluk, Sea Dayak (Iban), Land Dayak, Melanau, Temiar, Negritos. In a class or club of which you are a member, have each person pick an ethnic group to investigate. Use encyclopedias and other library resources to find out about how these people live and what they believe. Report your findings to your group.

3. The ethnic Chinese in Malaysia celebrate the Chinese New Year in late January or February. Each year is named after one of 12 animals in this order: Rat, Ox, Tiger, Rabbit, Dragon, Snake, Horse, Ram, Monkey, Rooster, Dog, Pig. Figure from 1987, the Year of the Rabbit, to find the animal of the year in which you were born. The Chinese believe you have the personality and character traits of that animal. What do you think? Use your imagination and books from the library on ethnic or religious holidays to come up with the animal traits. Figure out your parents' and brothers' and sisters' animals. Do you think *their* personalities seem to fit?

4. When Malaysia executed two Australian drug smugglers, some Western countries protested. Using recent periodicals from the library, find out what, if any, response your government had to the executions. Also compare the penalties of your government with those of Malaysia's for trafficking in illegal drugs. Discuss your findings with your class.

5. Think of an occupation or career that interests you. Would you be able to do this kind of work in Malaysia? Would being male or female make a difference? Would your ethnic background make a difference? Use sources of recent information from the library for your information.

More Things to Do — Activities

These projects are designed to encourage you to think more about Malaysia. They offer ideas for interesting group or individual projects that you can do at school or at home.

1. How does your life compare to Widiyati's? Write an imaginary letter to her. Explain how you are the same or different.

2. See if your town has any people from Vietnam. Invite one to your class to talk about the experience of coming to this country.

3. Here is a recipe for a Malaysian desert called *benkang pisang*. Be sure an adult is around to help out.

   1 cup (250 ml) milk
   2 bananas
   3½ cups (875 ml) flour
   1 tablespoon (15 ml) baking powder
   2 tablespoons (30 ml) instant coffee (undissolved)

   3 eggs
   ½ teaspoon (5 ml) salt
   ½ cup (125 ml) butter
   ½ cup (125 ml) brown sugar
   8" x 8" (20 cm x 20 cm) greased baking pan

Preheat oven to 350°F (180°C). Mix eggs and sugar, and beat until fluffy. Mash bananas and add milk and instant coffee. Beat butter until creamy. Mix flour, baking powder, and salt. Add banana mixture and flour mixture alternately to the butter, a little at a time. Add egg mixture and beat until the batter is smooth. Pour the batter into the greased pan. Bake for ½ - ¾ hour or until lightly brown on top. Serve warm or cool.

4. Why do you think it is important to study the history of Malaysia to understand it today?

5. If you would like a pen pal in Malaysia, write to these people:

International Pen Friends
P.O. Box 65
Brooklyn, New York 11229

Be sure to tell them what country you want your pen pal to be from. Also include your full name and address.

"Selamat tinggal!"

Index